FROM A FAR CORNER
An Anthology of Poetry from the Easternmost Reaches of Maine

FROM A FAR CORNER
An Anthology of Poetry from the Easternmost Reaches of Maine

THE PRIMAVERA PRESS
2018

From a Far Corner:
An Anthology of Poetry from the Easternmost Reaches of Maine
Copyright © 2018. All rights reserved. Please see Acknowledgements page at the end of this volume for permissions from previous publications.

Library of Congress Control Number: 2018935169

Requests for further permissions or information should be made to theprimaverapress@gmail.com.

Authors: Andrea Suarez Hill, Andrew A. Cadot, Anne Leaver, Dianna Ammons Johnson, Donald Crane, Gerald George, Gerard NeCastro, Grace Sheridan, Joanne Jacob, Kris Larson, Les Simon, Nancy Juretie, Nancy Tancredi, Patricia Marie Babin, Peter Anderson, Ray N. Beal, Sandra Woodward.

Cover Photo: Ray N. Beal

ISBN-13: 978-0-9894263-8-1
ISBN-10: 0-9894263-8-6

http://www.primaverapress.com

PREFACE

The stately Porter Memorial Library dates to 1893. Built of local granite in the Romanesque Revival style, it stands as a monument to pride in public architecture, in contrast to the later-day banality of the post-office structure across the street. People cared about buildings back then, it seems to say. What people sought inside mattered—books, magazines, newspapers, the stuff from which information is gathered, opinions are taken, views are debated, and pleasure is received. Important changes have come over the years: several computers inside offer access to the Internet, for example. But enlightenment for the mind and enjoyment for the imagination may still be found here. And the staunch statue of a Civil War soldier guards the way to its front door.

Through that door on the last Friday of every month, the Porter Poets, as we call ourselves, have trooped. We sit down around a couple of aging tables near the old fireplace to read our poems, hear poems from others, and offer both criticism and encouragement. Head Librarian Lee Downing promoted the group's formation, and sometimes sits in with us. Nothing about us is formal; anyone is a "member" who wants to take part. We come from Machias, Maine, the Washington County "shire town" where the library is located, but also from Addison, Beals Island, Cutler, East Machias, Jonesboro, Milbridge, Northfield, Roque Bluffs, and other towns on Washington County's coast.

You wouldn't expect much poetry from so remote a location. We live fewer than fifty miles from the Canadian border at the northeastern edge of the United States. Augusta, Maine's capital city, lies more than three times that distance from us, and Portland, the state's largest city, more than four. Small wonder that the poets in those towns have seldom heard of us. Yet poetry's power is evident even here where there are mostly trees. A poet seems to be scribbling behind every third fir and fourth maple. We're not creating cleverness, however. We have things to say. We speak them now to you.

For the Porter Poets
Gerald George

TABLE OF CONTENTS

CRASH

The fix kicked in
as he lay wide-eyed
between sand and a sky
high, broad and wide,
the sea invisible, just
an azure edge . . .

no Pacific sounds,
only his blood
pounding to leave
his skin behind
beneath a windshield
smashed to crystal web.

A shard sliced
this sailor's bicep and
a maroon Chinese dragon
bled mountains of myth
and benevolence
he sought to claim . . .

before the cobalt blue
Subaru collided with smack
and arranged a release
to soothe wounds
no one could reach.

— Andrea Suarez Hill

GONE

Strong, straight white-washed fences,
figures who knew their ground,
protected creatures and fell
forward together with posts
leaning toward each other
like old couples walk,
their boards now grey and moss covered,
shrunken past middle age
and scores of frosts.

Sunk in dung,
a couch to rest upon,
the manure spreader spreads
her wheels below
a steaming coverlet when once
she enjoyed greening fields
into summer forage with
an '86 Ford, its primer past to
rust, a doorless, floorless frame,
hollow as the hay loft
they once filled.

A barn sags like an old man
crooked on his cane,
the cracked and creaky sill.
The roof is swayed like backs
of horses who cruise pastures out of work,
waiting for a curry.
Its rafters are broken ribs that
protrude like hips
that groan when
wind blows cold while
the loft struggles to hold
a chaff and seed load.

Inside a tack room rots.
Tired boots, unpolished old soldiers
from horseshows past,

ankles broken, toes curled,
stand huddled beneath
bridles hung from pegs,
bits crusty with saliva,
leather reins stiff as
last rider's hands.

Ribbons red, yellow, blue,
two walls full, stretch above
cracked leather halters with
brass name plates gone green,
hung in homage to
those gone away before
cobwebs caught whinnies
echoed in empty stalls,
calling through a farm bowed
to years gone 'round.

— Andrea Suarez Hill

MOON SPINNER

From the river's bed
a moon sated and
silver crawls over the flats,
meets lead-red mud,
moves my horizon,
reshapes the shore,
unseats mauve skies
and slate grey clouds
above a drain tide
as a poem lets loose
with a pull words work
on gravity channeled
through an inner sea.

— Andrea Suarez-Hill

MARCH

March seventh, minus seven,
sea smoke white-washes sun,
    a ghost afloat ice
   near break up in bay.
 Boats, gulls, ducks, doze,
minutes morph to months,
     my mood slumps . . .

Mailboxes decorate dirt roads
  with fences plowed down,
saline sandstorms blind drivers
  on bumpy, broken, black tar,
road signs peek from snow banks
    like green shoots,
red squirrels run when fox pounce . . .

Fisher cats hiss in moonlight,
  deer chew cedar trees
    low with snow,
ravens' beaks pick and shovel
    communal crumbs
 and dent a glacial crown
  over sleepy, supple soil.

        — Andrea Suarez Hill

HALLOWED

A black woodstove gone gray with white heat,
claw marks of buried dogs on worn pine floor,
impressions of first words written on a cherry desk,
obits stuck in decayed books like prayer cards in purse pockets
beside a crinkled image of a colt, bred, grown and gone
with hoof beats that echoed in the pasture:

Each a knot tied in the heart that slows its flow
like a fence reframes movement of a once wild life
forced to travel trapped in borders
cut by seasons after the summery sun falls
and sends shadow farther down the hill
until All Hallows when the dead walk unfrayed,
again golden amid green days.

— Andrea Suarez Hill

DREAMCATCHER

Thick as heavy cream,
fog hugged the sun
above the bay, tight
as the armor of night
held close a dreamer . . .

dressed to kill critics
a harem of hypocrites,
formed long black lines,
a gauntlet of double edged
cold comments so sharp
each cut a plank in reason . . .

'she felt a funeral in her brain,'
the barbed words chosen
to cut bone, but
flags blown to bright bits,
prayers pinned to a line,
cut mourning's damp doom . . .

and a new moon rode
low over the dream's cape,
a narrow blade
that cut the string
between night and day.

— Andrea Suarez Hill

PASSAGE

The title page of summer always opened to
Lee standing like Mercator's titan
atop a flatbed truck with
five hundred bales framed by
the weight of light blue,
sky he held with the sun
on his shoulders, a tank top
showing his farmer's tan.
From his paws like rough sawn boards
flew each fifty pounds of fodder
while we ground crew scattered and hopped
quick to sweat as chaff filled floor and shirt.

Good hay turned the heavens
on their axis until he stumbled
and broke his.
Now beneath white light, Atlas endures in
frosted glass quarters full of quiet noise,
the blunt poetry of I.C.U
punctuated by ventilator pings, whispers,
paper shuffled, the swish of yellow gowns
and rubber soles like the soft sound
his footsteps made on last Fall's hunting ground.

A monitor's metallic eyes replaced deer in his sights,
and jagged green lines on a screen track blood and being.
Around the family farm house
tractor, tedder, and baler waited since fields were high
but he never again will bind with rough twine
well dried grass stuffed tight morning 'til night.
The machines were brokered to highest bidders
with the F 250 and a used RV.
Alone, the side-by-side swings in wind
filled with fallen yellow leaf.

— Andrea Suarez Hill

A PRAYER FOR THE LAST DECADE

If I survive to eighty-five,
I can expect to not remember much
of the last ten years with Parkinson's
as the hours and days leave
a trail of broken synapses.
An early trip across the Styx
is one choice but would be unwise:

I'd miss the swamp maple in the Fall,
the smell of smoke from an applewood fire,
the smile on the face of a familiar friend,
the silky touch of a retriever's ears,
the taste of Thanksgiving turkey
with a glass of chablis.

My hope is to be patient,
to greet each new event or loss
without judgment,
denial, or desire for a different day.

May I greet each
as if for the first time,
though it may be the last.

— Andrew A. Cadot

CREATIVITY

can still be cultivated
in old age
with practice and meditative down time —
despite the wear and tear
on all the wires that allow
insights to be installed.

But synapses in the brain
are broken by Parkinson's Disease —
dopamine is destroyed
before it can be delivered.
The path of words winds down
into a cul-de-sac,
so new ideas can't cross
the gulf because the bridge is out.

Yet no death sentence is delivered:
One can choose to press on,
to persevere
in the belief that time
and levadopa may still allow
new poems to emerge
across the chasm.

— Andrew A. Cadot

LIVING WILL

If you should find me
in a hospital bed
after a Parkinson's fall —
please do what you can
to allow me to move on
without tubes or ventilators
to keep me artificially alive.

With less than a decade left
before I start to lose
one by one, my marbles,
the use of my car, clubs, and computer,
my strong preference is to exit early,
rather than be overcharged
to be resuscitated at every surly turn.

I will not want to stick around
to endure a private hell
without a fully functioning brain
when my face no longer smiles,
my eyes blink once for yes
twice for no, to a nurse I don't recognize.

If what is left is a poor
imitation, I pray for a pass
to seek heaven on the other shore.

— Andrew A. Cadot

STAR

It is quiet now.
Late sun reddens
the sea torn birch
in the woods along the bluff.

All day storm clouds gathered to the north
darkening the walls
along the orchard
gone feral and bitter with withered apples
that sweetened only with the frost.
Late-born geese feed
in long shadows into their own dusk
born too late to migrate.

My unborn child is dead.
I cannot breathe.
It is almost night and a few small stars are twinkling.

— Anne Leaver

THE CLAMMERS

The tide was out half a mile, or more.
Mid-March and clammers bent double
like oil drills, shining wet
amongst great stones.
Light strained across the mud flats – purple-edged, shell pearl.
Two men, their knee-high boots and work coats, dusked
in the colors of mud and air, shimmered
in mist that gelled their skin. Slat crates scraped behind them
sinking, pulling free, and sinking.

They called back and forth in voices they had always known,
as if they had dug in these flats
their lives. I couldn't hear the words
swallowed in water that chipped at frozen rocks.

— Anne Leaver

The Old House

The old house snaps and thumps as cold sinks deeper
into timbers. Here and there a tassel of ice jingles
from the lips of a window. The cat yawns. The dog
flexes his toes and yips in a dream. A housefly
bats into a wall, a door, the empty ash can. A truck
passes on the road tapping tire studs against macadam.
Across the river, the forest's edge: a canticle winds through
the trees, high notes shrill then muffle. Firs bow
and rise in the dark breeze. Everything is settled.

— Anne Leaver

LAST GULL

As the bay lowers, surf pulls at jasper stones
rolling them smooth with a basso rasp
like thunder passing between clouds.

Here on these western banks of Fundy cold water steams
mingling with sky, dreaming alive
a dance of sea smoke that tears in wisps
like spider webs torn and wet with fog
fingering through the goose tongued grass
that grows to the water's edge
and wild rose that scars already fissured cliffs.

These waters wander back toward the moon by day, by month
pulling round the ocean like some glaucoma of sea.

Time eludes here. In the fog, the sun
without direction, lights and leaves
and nights pass, barely darker with the northern moon
that orchestrates some ululating glow beyond vision.

I have become what I fear most:
that woman cold and inconsolable as stone.
Tonight low tide at one. In the nimbus of the moon
waning, day's last gull scries the empty sky.

I cannot see her, tipping the horizon.

— Anne Leaver

THE BARDO OF THE CUTLER ROAD

Sunday:
I am wondering how to say what it is I have to say.

Something like:
every culture lives its sex and dung and death its own way.

In beloved France it's all in the street:
Walker beware.
In Canada, deep frozen, no error.
On US rural routes,

oh, what can I say
I'm crazy from living alone.

Fact is, this is a forgotten place, and any life
left out in a night meets death
and if not death, demolition, hideous end
and tender evacuation.

I trekked out early, pockets packed
with plastic veggie sacks like petite body bags.
Searched the edge of wild bergamot
for dog turds left the day and days before.

And there
in the violent, twilit silence
churning upon my dog's dung
the slugs of the Cutler Road curled,
with gourmand audacity, over remains, without judgment,
grateful, unperturbed,

luscious in their golden flesh.

— Anne Leaver

FORGOTTEN BLOOD

If I could see the black sea
It would be darker
Than the aurora absent and
Imaged in the back sky over the shed
That leans into the trampled path of mallow
Edging into the January woods

Sometimes we sit up late
Telling the secrets
Of old dogs and childhood ghosts
And children left in rafters
Filled with camphor
Now glazed in dust and down
Of pillows dreamed cloud-like

Who is listening in the wind
Flute-like in the old birch
Or the curl of bark whistling back
Or shrilling in periwinkle shells
Remembered in pockets sticky now with salt
And coats hung by the back door?

There is a photo of Ireland
West, where my greats bore the grands
And there is Baltimore and Ballina and
Cities of forgotten blood
Pressed in photo paper
Sparkling in the dark

But what holds me is the hairline fissure
Along the ceiling beam
Is the memory of his hand
His voice, like the snore of the ocean
Lulling the sepulchral note
Of the lost and lost and lost

— Anne Leaver

THE STONING

How small
the city looks from here
as if, if I
could hold my hand
so (posing in offering)
it might fit into my palm.
How small and grey, how without meaning.
      I saw her,
weaving in and out of doors and cars and quickly turning back to smile
into the long waves of auburn sun that bristled out, sometimes, in little
strokes of air along the harbor.
      She had always been as if a memory,
a leaf dropped at the edge of the pond,
like a moment, a thought that shattered when the phone rang.
      He stooped down, and with his finger wrote on the ground,
She was never of consequence, a timid wind, drawn through an eye;
      I saw her
shorn, then skinless, translucent. And when she fell, a sound like carriage
horses clattered over asphalt and circled her
and cheers of crowds surrounded her
where he held up her hair like a trophy. She looked out of a future gone
and saw him smile, and widely jeer; and the stones fell silent and white.
      And again he stooped down, and wrote on the ground, this:
city of no consequence,
woman,
photo,
stones.

— Anne Leaver

WINNOWING

A dark scar seared across the pages of human history
Records the sum of each individual's contribution
To our path of violence

In the beginning, violence forged the way toward survival
The revelation of our slow, halting emergence from that legacy
Suggests there can be better angels of our nature[1]

As if the future breathes a new life
Blowing aside the useless chaff
Exposing a deeper core of who we might become

Predation, lust, shamans, and coercion dissipate
Revealing comfort and promise in cooperation; joy in partnerships with
    loved ones
Opening windows to spiritual freedom and individual choice[2]

Like-minded, we winnow through our cacophonous thoughts
To share the found treasures
Of understanding and peace[3]

A May basket woven with string theory; luxuries of satin and October love
Shelters for squirrels and encounters with elk in the night;
Filigreed shawls for departing winter

And yes, lullabies of Auschwitz[4]

[1] Abraham Lincoln; [2] Stephen Pinker; [3] Elie Wiesel; [4] Porter Poets`

— Dianna Ammons Johnson

UNCOVERING

Walking the cobblestone streets near Istanbul University
He moves with a loose swagger
In his wake, a covered female figure
He progresses without a backward glance
Confident of her shadow following

After several more strides he becomes aware she has stumbled
Falling head-long on the rough stones
Folds of black fabric flare
Exposing the full extent of her bare legs, pale and plump
In the bright sunlight of the street

Rather than turn away as modesty would expect
I watch this brief moment of glaring vulnerability
As the husband turns in annoyance to attend his wife's recovery
The shroud now re-enveloping her
Erasing her form

This scene unfolds
Beneath large, bright posters
Proclaiming recruitment opportunities at the University
Plastered with images of eager and unguarded faces
Of the young women students.

— Dianna Ammons Johnson

SWEET BARTER

On my grandfather's farm
The end-of-summer air dripped with sticky sweetness
Steaming from black boiling cauldrons
Thin yellow juice of the sugar cane thickening to amber

Begun as fragile sprigs piercing the red dirt hills
Demanding cruel sweltering work
Through oven-hot days
To nurture the explosion of thick shafts

Ending with the hack and slash of machetes
Fallen canes, jack-strawed
Curiously purple and pale green
Gathered up in muscular arms and brought to the syrup mill

The grind stone in its crushing anger
Consumed the canes
Fed by men quick and agile
Yet accustomed to inevitable wounds and blistering scars

The stone was turned in its trough by a cussed mule
Responding singularly to the seeming cruelty of my grandfather
A clever, common-sense man
Who contrived the completely self-sufficient operation

For this yearly ritual, friends and kin gathered as bees to the final distillate
The young ones, myself among them
Corralled at a protective distance but jostling for the front line
To see tantalizing dangers played out for real

With frightened fascination
We crunched samples of pealed and sliced cane between our teeth
Squeezing out a sugary antidote
Against scary scalding nightmares that might come

The final molten essence
Poured in a viscous stream
Into rows of waiting tin buckets then sealed with a flat lid
A southern currency to be sold, bartered and gifted

Sixty years hence
It all bubbles to the edge of my consciousness
As liquid memory
A single succulent drop on the tongue

— Dianna Ammons Johnson

HOLDING ON

I must have been about eight in that picture; one of three kids with a fish so big it took all of us to hold it up dangling from a pole hoisted on one end by my older brother Robert, who balanced it with much effort, elbow to his waist and a bit of swagger in his wide stance, wearing his much prized high-topped tennis shoes and trying to appear aloof; baby brother Kenneth in the middle, arms reaching far above his head stretching his suspenders and his little fists pushing up resolutely on the pole like a weight lifter; then the fish; then barefoot me in my most favorite blue jean skirt I'm leaning very close to the fish, nearly touching the gaping mouth while awkwardly balancing my end of the pole; the three of us holding on together, perhaps trying to hold on still; but looking smug about it then, showing off the catfish Daddy caught in Lanana Creek and brought home like a trophy, as if we had — at least for that one moment — the whole world in our shared grasp.

— Dianna Ammons Johnson

BELONGING

Have you ever seen a solitary loon
Fly so close overhead that you could all but feel
The wind from its slow, deliberate wing beats?

Did an elongated sunset play itself out
Over a smooth surfaced lake
Reflecting the closing progression of white - gold - pink?

Was the evening stillness split apart
By the loon's quavering call
In affirmation of your singular place in this sure and lovely wildness?

Would you stand quietly and let this moment
Explain your obstinate, unflinching bond to things that are real
To the dimming sky, the quiet lake, the cry of the loon?

— Dianna Ammons Johnson

YOUR SIDE OF THE BED

On the nightstand, curlers,
cotton balls, a dried out lipstick,
a mild mystery novel, several
unguents I don't know
the uses of.

And in the bed itself,
still the impress of your
hip and shoulder (or is it
my imagination).

It's been a year
nevertheless - - half
asleep - - I s-l-i-d-e my hand
along under the blankets,

But meet only air.

— Donald Crane

15A AND 15B
FAIRVIEW COURT

Begonias and lilies

A recipe for pecan divinity

The length of veil
On this spring's bonnet

All deadly weapons

In the war between
The misses Patience Witherspoon
And Abigail Brown

— Donald Crane

Packing For The Trip

Taking sunsets

Spring rain

Swallows overhead
       against a dome of blue

My little granddaughter
       in her First Communion
       dress

My wife on the morning
       of our wedding day

Leaving my sorrows
       to entertain themselves.

          — Donald Crane

OLD MAN

The old man shuffles
about the lawn, following
his cane - - - step

Pause

Step

Pause

Step

And glancing now and then
at his little great granddaughter,
tumbling with her ball.

"Hard to believe we belong
to the same species," he mutters
half aloud

But then each stoops
to pick a wild flower.

— Donald Crane

DANCE

Grandmother danced for me
   in the kitchen
To an old, old tune on
   the radio.
She said it was her favorite
   when she was growing up.

Then she collided
   with the table, knocking off
   a dainty porcelain tea cup.
It was the last of the set
   from HER grandmother's
   wedding.

We stared in horror at the little pile
   of slivers.
Then she winked at me, scooped up
   my Teddy Bear and, cradling him
   in her arms, whirled away.

I never told mom.

          — Donald Crane

EAGLES

I first heard
Beethoven's Ninth
When I was a boy

Now 81, I recalled that moment
This morning

When no less than seven eagles
Came in with the tide

And swung in mile wide circles
Over the fast filling bay.

— Donald Crane

IOWA

It's Sunday, and the annual
outdoor baptism and picnic
of the Downer's Corner Baptist Church.

Little Francine Stottelmeyer stands
waist deep in Poplar Creek - - - which
as always is laden with prairie
silt - - - in a white gown made by
her mother from a piece of percale saved
since Francine was a baby.

Her gown is empire waisted with
an embroidered hem and tied
with a pink satin sash that floats
fetchingly out behind on
the surface.

Beside her in the muddy water
is old man MacDonald in a frayed
white shirt and suspenders last worn
at his second wife's funeral.

Those inclined to comment - - - and there
are some in every congregation - - -
whisper that the old man has decided
not to take any chances.

Arlene Stottlemeyer, who is 17 and
considered very sensitive, swears
she hears a meadowlark
on a nearby fence rail
explode in a hallelujah of congratulation
as her younger sister emerges gasping
and sputtering from the murk.

Afterward, there is fried chicken,
cucumber and potato salad, lemonade,
and three kinds of pie.

The men pitch horse shoes, but not too strenuously
considering the day; while their wives
cluster together exchanging recipes
and baby news; and the children hunt
tadpoles in the reeds along the creek,
their go-to-meetin' shoes and socks
in a neat row on the bank.

— Donald Crane

THE HOSPITAL ROOM

Two weeks after
    Admission

When the mists are finally
    beginning to dissipate

I realize that someone
    with a mop

Smiles at me
    every day.

          — Donald Crane

SALT WATER FARM

Aunt Beede is up before six to make
her husband his breakfast of corn meal
cakes and syrup before he takes the boat
out to tend his weir in Little Neck Cove.

Then she sweeps down the floor
and sets the big copper clothes boiler
going on the stove.

After she milks the cow and feeds
the chickens it's time to wring out
the clothes and hang them out to dry.

Next she fetches flour and salt from the pantry
and milk, butter, and a lump of yeast from
the cooler suspended in the well and
works up the dough for the week's baking.

By then it is near noon; she makes
a quick lunch standing at the stove
and spooning up soup from the pot that's
always simmering at the back of the range.

If the clothes aren't dry for ironing yet
she takes her big ash handled hoe
and scratches around the potato vines
in the garden.

At 2:30 it's time to haul wood for
the stove. But before that she settles
herself wearily in the old rocker by
the window ("just a moment - - - mind")

And gazes out over the bay where
the little waves, sparkling like
diamonds under the sun, make
a brilliant, unattainable fairy land.

— Donald Crane

NIMSHIK'S DOG

Behold! Nimshik lectured
on the Life of the Mind to an audience
of the middling literati
glomming on every word
(Nimshik was that good!),
when—*woof, woof!*—
Nimshik's faithful dog
got loose in the lecture hall,
barreled to the lectern, and,
ears flapping, tongue lapping,
flipped Nimshik up in the air
—*ka-boom!*—and back
on the floor on his butt,
papers flying skyward,
then descending upon him
as he wondered whatever
in the wide, wide world
accounted for this upset:

> The dog felt love for Nimshik?
> The dog felt eager to be free?
> The dog felt desire for dinner?
> The dog wished to hog the stage?
> The collar of the dog gave way?
> The strain on the chain made it burst?
> The atmosphere was intense?
> The lecture was too intense?
> The hall was too supercharged?
> *What was the mutt doing there anyway?*

The audience oohed and awed and ran out,
breaking loose from the Life of the Mind,
which lay in notes around the floor
where Nimshik sat, suddenly shouting:
"Kill that damned dog!"

And then he stopped.
And thought.

And realized.
The Life of the Mind would not behave this way.
The Life of the Mind would be calm.
It would just get up.
It would recapture the dog.
It would reassemble the papers.
It would apologize for the interruption.
(Yes, do not forget that.)
And then it would continue on.
It would use the damned dog
(that is, "the unexpected event")
to illustrate the Great Truth
that the Life of the Mind would reassert
control.
That brought the audience back.
They sheepishly re-sought their seats.
They sat quietly through the rest of the lecture.
They felt really bad.
("Damn the dog, anyway.")
They felt they had betrayed
the Life of the Mind.

— Gerald George

CAN'T

the circus now grinds andante
suffering stale machinery

much plied though in good repair
and the animals saleable

but without its misplaced tent
the boundary comes down

makes one sense the coming
of a can't of shattered matter

scattering all over
like artificial snow

— Gerald George

AFTER THE FROST

In the last minutes of
one of those bright October afternoons
when one thousand three hundred twenty-one
shades of green
are mining their closets
for the perfect outfit for heading
                                    south

and making their last visits to the twenty-nine greens
that will stay behind for the colder months,

you,
            skittling past papery grape leaves
                (hiding their age spots in their curled fingers)
            arcing over long-legged snapdragons
                (lifting their heads pleasantly above their dowager's humps)
bend low and snip a slim stem of pink mallow
                (one of few not fallen and lost among the debris of
                        summer's orgy),
rise up, and, ignoring the memo your sacroiliac has sent you,
            find five golden raspberries,
                bulging with nano-oceans of sweetness and desire.

Like a Forty-Niner beaming with the discovery of a new vein,
            you bring to me,
                introducing peas to the company of kale and spinach
                        already on the table,
            your precious lode,

            which from one another's fingers we taste
                not the brash overstated brushstrokes of a blazing
midsummer frolic,
                but the subtle intricate collage of an incandescent October
                love.

                — Gerard NeCastro

COLUMBUS DAY IN LITTLE ITALY
ERIE, PENNSYLVANIA

An hour after a crew of men with arms carved from the mast of a flagship pound iron stakes into an ocean of asphalt, they hoist three green, red, and white tents, like the sails of the Santa Maria filled with the humid August air, high above the white hair of Filomena Caviccio and Joe DiVeccchio, friends since first grade at Columbus School, two blocks away, the same year they received their First Communion at St. Paul's Church, thirty yards away.

A week later, on the morning after the Assumption (The Ferragosto di Santa Maria, as Father Marini used to call it), after five hundred gallons of pasta e fagioli, ninety-two thousand strands of spaghetti, three thousand cannoli, and a quarter million smiles have crossed the lips of immigrants to this tiny temporary village, Joe and his grandchildren, Sarah, Izzie, Shakira, and little Joe watch the sails of the tents fall, and Joe tucks his Italians-Make-Better-Lovers apron and his mushroom-shaped chef's hat under his arm and waves with his other arm, the one with the USS Pennsylvania tattoo on its bicep, to Filomena: "Arrivederci!"

Columbus Day, two months later, USPS carrier Gertrude Schwartz, sipping the last of her Peroni in the mid-afternoon silence, flips past Apocalypse Now to highlights of the Redskins-Patriots game (a massacre), thinks about the mail she does not need to deliver today on the 400 block of 16th Street to Parker, Placidi, Rodriguez, Kim, Nez, and St. Paul's, and, savoring the last olive from her antipasto, remembers that she needs to pick up her daughter from the Melting Pot Day Care Center at the old Knights of Columbus Hall.

— Gerard NeCastro

FOOD FOR THOUGHT

On a July Sunday afternoon
  Designed for iced lemonade and slightly swaying hammocks,
    You lay your soft black head,
    Still abundant with winter's growth—
      Rich as the mouton stole Aunt Mary wore
      On her Christmas visit, that white morning when
      She squeezed my yeasty cheeks and intoned,
        "When you start school,
        The nuns are going to eat you up"
      And I pictured a rounder, more Italian version of Hansel
        Surrounded by smiling women in black,
            With forks—
  On my curved pale bare foot,
    Aching from my weekly campaign
    To bring order to
    God's little green chaos.

As my cramps melt under your warm fur blanket
  And I ask myself if your gesture signifies thirteen years of trust
    Or the fact that my foot is where you want your head to be
You wake and shift your head
  Back to the flat padded area rug,
And I recall Sister Concetta in her black miracle of a habit
  Waking us too soon from our afternoon kindergarten nap:
    "God wants us to be well rested and fed for battle, not lazy"
And ask you why, but you, silent, do not answer,
    "Your foot wasn't comfortable,"
    "I didn't want to wear out my welcome," or
    "All pleasure, old man, is fleeting."

Instead, like a lioness beginning to gnaw your fresh kill
  Or a saintly nurse tending a wounded soldier,
    You lick my foot,
    And I wonder.

        — Gerard NeCastro

SEVEN LEAVING

Autumn frost, fourth night:
Wild ones whisper, break loose, drop:
Maple leaves skitter.

Escapees delight,
In darkness, twin beams catch them
Crossing Shady Lane.

Last comes Red, limping;
Finds sudden solid chill below
A chance truck's blind tire.

Onto neighbors' lawns
Six stumble, breathless, heaving;
Mourn their fated friend.

Two were raked at dawn;
Three mulched in noontime sun;
One's still on the run.

— Gerard NeCastro

ROSE IS RED, BUT VIOLET IS NOT

"Pale, hard, dry, she found me here,
Her favorite forgotten little sister.

I saw, heard, smelled, she was sick,
Her hips flat, flabby, not the Rose I knew.

She was a wild Irish thing,
And every man — one too many man,

Sang of her dawn-like fingers.
She wanted, though, one perfect limousine.

Clothes second-hand, hair yellow,
She rambled to Texas and married oil.

But soon, all past, no future,
Her hopes were buried beneath snow, bitter.

Rust eyes, pale mosaic skin.
I fed her well. Showed pictures: her, me, and —

She slept a hundred winters,
In spring, cheeks red and white, her bloom returned.

Too much bloom. Too damn much bloom."

So she thought, Rose's sister, Violet,
Blue hair, knuckles like smoothed chunks of granite,
Scraping the red, red clay from her shovel,
Washing her hands, noting the June sunset
And familiar boots, 12-D, up the path,
And clearing photo scraps from the table,

Where, with patient fingers and crisp scissors,
She'd pruned, until three faces became two.

— Gerard NeCastro

AFTER EL FARO

Were it my only sister
fed to the sea, (or swallowed
by clambering cancer cells,
or found in a deathly doze
three hundred miles away
in her cat-clawed wingback chair),

when the unwanted arrives
packaged in tears,
will my distress
skim the surface
like a rainy day road
that dries overnight,

or, when the unseemly
screams for justice
will grief surge
as a hurricane-wrought
Atlantic that rocks itself
even in the calm?

Will I sorrow more
for absence of presence
or for singular rememberings,
fingered one by one
dangling like fringe
on the afghan she crocheted:

    bread pudding with raisins
    in Momma's poppy bowl,

    the scraping in the cellar
    when Dad shoveled coal,

    newspaper for a blanket
    while napping on the floor?

Why mourn at all, I ask,

for that which cannot be retrieved,
the sunken and the void; yet,
plunge we must into depths of loss
until comfort seeps within,
and saturates the marrow.

— Grace Sheridan

SIMEON

Drawn
to Jerusalem's temple
eyes darting, ears alert

then,
the infant Jesus
enfolded in his arms:

tenderly
search for features
as any devoted one might

discern
a holy essence
beyond humanity

see
at last, Oh,
Sovereign Lord

see
at last
Your Promised Light.

— Grace Sheridan

PRIME TIME

So what if Shakespeare wrote sonnets
— let *The Merchant of Venice* sprawl
face down under the ottoman —

dive into Nachos
slathered with gooey cheese
gulp Irish Rose

no one to hear him belch
spew up hollow nights
swallowed with televised crime

gunshots putting the skids
to a deal gone wrong
zombie on a dead end road

missing the connection
packing on the pounds.

— Grace Sheridan

THE GALA

cored, sliced
lengthwise, then
diagonally
on the nutmeg
dusted cutting board,
will fill the weighted glass
and while it heats
for twenty-two seconds
in the microwave,
I slice a curl
of cheddar
which will rest
on top when
placed beside
the small tined fork
on the gold colored
placemat for my mini
feast with gratitude
for orchards laden
with jewels like stars
within reach.

— Grace Sheridan

COATS I HAVE KNOWN

after Ted Berrigan

Ethel Bacon's slim black woolen
  worn as long
    as all the Sundays I knew her.

The double-breasted camel hair,
  pearl-buttoned tab on the center back
    that Lois and Jackie sported
      when it was collegiate style.

A hand-me down mouton lamb
  Mother thought too lavish,
    but cozy for nuzzling
      my nose on a frosty night.

The sleek white vinyl with
  imitation lion's mane when Carlene
    was in her Hollywood phase.

Dad's scratchy herringbone, solemn
  as funerals or church, softened
    by butterscotch candy loose as a button
      deep in the right side pocket.

My tailored brushed-blue-wool: shawl collar,
  raglan sleeves, shoulder darts arrayed
    like a scallop shell across the back,
      satin lining hugging
        luxury to myself.

— Grace Sheridan

AGE OF IGNORANCE

> "Get a lift with a Camel"
> —R. J. Reynolds Tobacco Company

Famous explorer, Mrs. William LaVarre,
coughs, lights another cigarette,
wonders if she might have gone too far.
Is there anything she will regret?
The model does resemble her, she knows
the rifle's real, although the leopard's not.
Deep-sea diver Crilley puffs and blows
out the smoke, says they "hit the spot."
It's January, nineteen thirty-five.
The ad in *The New Yorker* makes it clear —
Camels "turn your steam on," you'll derive
energy, feel alert, full of cheer.
> Benchley, Thurber, Aiken, Langston Hughes
> share the space with cigarettes and booze.

— Joanne Jacob

DISASSEMBLY OR FALLING APART

How many days did it take us to build that shed?
Directions made it clear that there were four
hundred little nuts and bolts and washers
in plastic baggies. We supplied the tools.
For fifteen years that tin withstood the winds,
rain, hail and snow which assailed it,
housed bags of soil, fertilizer,
wheelbarrow, secateurs and pots.
Covered with a tarp, in one corner,
bundles of leftover insulation.
Then lately I observed a bulging side.
The door was off its track and unsecured.
In dire straits the roof caved in and died.
At last the shed succumbed to Nature's scorn.
It had to go. They took it down in pieces.
I wonder where the squirrels and mice will shelter?

— Joanne Jacob

BARBER SHOP 1960

No fuss, no crying, not a sign of fear —
        his face composed as though he knew the drill —
his calm demeanor — all this made it clear
        that something special, not against his will,
        was coming into play as he sat still.
His father took some photos (we're all there).
Did his brother wonder, was he then aware?

Glass bottles, tins of talc stood behind
        our barber, lone employee of the shop,
whose manner, smile and patience proved him kind.
        The scissors paused, then made its final chop,
        and the child got his reward — a lollipop.
Today they go to stylists for a trim,
sometimes grow their beards on a whim.

— Joanne Jacob

BLACK DRESS

A crowd assembles on a fateful day,
tears on some, solemn faces all.
Chatter stops, as though they must obey
the man appearing now — regal, tall.
Another century — some miles away —
the girl stands up, ignoble, stature small.
She's chosen, for this speech, a long black dress.
"Four score and seven years . . . ." You know the rest.

— Joanne Jacob

"THE SPIRIT OF THE MARSH"
—granite sculpture by Lise Becu, 2011

Enveloped in the heron's plumage, she
looks out with half-closed eyes beyond the gates;
serene, as though resigned to her sad fate
to be land-locked, to never feel the sea
stream through her tresses, mournful elegy
(surely destined to replace those late
siren songs acclaimed by Wilde and Yeats)
accompanied by the wind in minor key.
With softest feathers he absorbs her grief,
with large wings gives strength to her resolve;
both eyes open to marsh, river, sky,
settling sometimes on trees bare of leaf,
nudging with his long bill to involve
her in new life, sheltered, as they lie.

— Joanne Jacob

POEM FOR ZEBULUN
LYING BETWEEN MY SHOULDER BLADES

I don't have wings,
nor can I grow any.

But I can hear you purring,
feel your bearable weight,
the coinage
of your companionship.

Otherwise I would,
if I could,
carry you
to some feline Elysium
where the clouds are mice
and you can chase them
all day.

— Kris Larson

**POEM FOR ZEBULUN AND ASHER
LYING ON MY CHEST**

You're
the two little
Triumph Spitfires
and I'm the Mack truck
hauling you off
to market
where
some diligent entrepreneur
or discerning princess
will take you in.

Then
I'll drive away,
not with a cigar
in my mouth
but with a halo of smoke
over my head
as if I had.

— Kris Larson

Last Dream

"I'll sail my ship alone, With all the dreams I own, Drifting out across the ocean blue."
(From *I'll Sail My Ship Alone* — 1950 song written by Moon Mullican a.k.a. Morry
Burns, Henry Bernard a.k.a. Henry Glover, Lois Mann a.k.a Sydney Nathan, and Henry
Thurston. Popularized by Moon Mullican. Also performed by Hank Williams, Sr., and
many others.)

Walking on from here, I come to that place in the woods off the road,
and check it out, trying to remember when I found this spot. Memory
slips into elder-hood, and in this thicket of scrubby scratching bushes,
I have to be with it awhile, nurturing my thoughts, prompt them from
my squat form supine among these towering and fallen majestic nobles.
Cradled in wooded wisdoms of white pines, maples, cedars, birches, oaks,
I should be more humbled.

Time fleets or crawls, depending on that ever changing point of view,
and slowly it comes to me in fitful flashes from the deepest recesses
as though in a fast fading dream upon awakening. I've dreamed here
before in this very spot on countless occasions, rather wistful dreams of
grace, fulfillment, and lasting happiness. The dream pervades once again,
this time in a plea to acknowledge not only what is, but that which is not.
Oh, those haunting wishes!

Something familiar has a hold on me, a grip tightening around my heart
that once knew the meaning of life rejoiced in the throes of love, that once
welcomed the good but never the evil gouging out these trenches in my soul.

Something else prods me upright, an endeavor more pathetic than I dreamed
possible. A restful spot this. Having stumbled upon it once more is fortuitous,
an opportunity to embrace, without judgement, those spirited memories again
reborn in this last dream.

— Les Simon

EARLY MORNING

With a new day coming on strong,
Chasing away last night's shadows,
Shedding light on subjects yet to be discovered,

Brightening faded hopes,
Revealing Earth's oft ignored riddles,
Warming chilled winds hailing from stone hearts,

Exposing foul deeds,
Evaporating dreams,
Distilling impatience,

Adorning the pious, the zealot, the hateful, the loving,
Illuminating the arena of war and peace,
Energizing those petty feuds with no quarter in sight,

I roam about in finite circles, blinded by the light.

— Les Simon

MEANWHILE

Opinions once placed Earth at the center
of the Solar System. Oh, wait, someone said,
that's not right, Earth rotates 'round the Sun.
Meanwhile,

Pursuits of Progress lay siege to happier pursuits,
insist on ambitious leaps into the Future
to instill an indispensable impression.
Meanwhile,

Juno, in just five years, locates Jupiter,
makes for big news, goes into orbit seeking
water and minerals (for some nefarious reason).
Meanwhile,

Itsy bitsy particles zip through accelerators,
controversy be damned, circulating indifference
across expanses already spoiled.
Meanwhile,

DNA researchers have climbed from the trenches
bearing a cause for aggressive tendencies, name it,
in their brilliance, the "Aggressive Gene."
Meanwhile,

In another field of exuberant minds, certain levels
of the neurotransmitter dopamine are declared
the culprit responsible for dominant personalities.
Meanwhile,

Imprudent incentives fire up the flow of dopamine,
embolden those tagged with the Aggressive Gene
to prevent opposition at every turn, at any cost.
Meanwhile,

Earth TILTS, wobbles out of control.

— Les Simon

A SEA OF DANDELIONS

Ventured out the other night once the storm
had somewhat settled down, found my way into
and all the way 'round the front yard.

Shuffled over fallen leaves, fallen wet leaves
of reddish golds clinging to Earth beneath
a Sanguine Moon waxing Gibbous, the
twinkle twinkle of clearing October skies
and dropping temperatures.

Waded through a sea of dandelions, firm
in their stubbornness to remain rooted,
prodigious and persistent at foiling efforts
to off the dudes once the delights in those
exquisite blossoms have been supped.

Oh, but what delicate leafy tastes they offer
if savored before bitterness sets in, brutal
to the surprised palate expecting something
far less consequential.

Now isn't that just the way of expectations,
            and dandelions,
teasing the overreaching intellect always
on the prowl for something more reliable,
more substantial, more encouraging than
a world overrun with puff balls.

— Les Simon

A DARK DAY AT LIME ROCK

i

it's dark, raining hard, lightning
the engines revving, roaring
waiting
hot, i point to the lime seltzer on
display
– one of these, please
– oh, sorry we are out, she smiles
– well, how about this one?
me still pointing
– no, we don't have any more
her still smiling, serious
– but what about this one here?
myself yet again, surprisingly calm,
       and surprisingly calm with the
same pleasing smile
she repeats *herself*, yet again
– we are out of those
– you can sell him that one
her dark-haired coworker says
       looking good
from behind the scenes
saving us both, each from the
american other
– with ice, please
i smile
they smile
everybody.

ii

the rain slows
the lime seltzer goes in quick gulps
thunder and lightening withdraws
unbiased
– rain tires only, comes the call

va-room! va-room!
wheels spinning over slick surfaces
moisture vaporizing, rising
sticking to everything
lap speeds and gas fumes also rising
more cornering problems
more spin-outs
more missed apexes
more gravel flying
dinging helmets and drivers' egos
track's drying,
– slick tires okay now!
away flies number forty-nine
lap speeds dropping . . .
tenth of a second
quarter of a second
a full second
three seconds!
testing over
no winners, no losers
nobody hurt, no damages
everybody hot, sticky,
and smiling.

— Les Simon

ALONE

Inside my house, I happened to see, through my vestibule window, a blue truck in my driveway behind my car.

Backing down the hallway, I moved aside to be out of potential sight.

Soon loud pounding, without stopping, attacked my front door and me, leaving me terrified.

Creeping back down the hall as flat as I could be against the wall and beyond, I reached my bed and lay down, shaking in fear.

My bell by the front door had been ignored.

Louder, more incessant pounding, with both fists and without a space inbetween, crashed into my ears.

Next my vestibule window began taking the beating. It's going to break!

Then a bright light streamed through the door, then the vestibule. I could see it searching the floor, ceiling, walls, slowly, before moving on. Oh God.

Quiet. The light moved into my bathroom and into the hallway through the open door.

I watched with only my eyeballs moving, my bed on the same plane, but the light would not be able to reach me.

As the light moved slowly I imagined it searching my tub, the toilet, both near the large picture window looking out to the woods beyond.

Quiet. Waiting. Getting out of bed without a sound, I crept to the hallway and looked through the vestibule window.

The truck was still there.

— Nancy Juretie

PIECES OF PAPER

from anywhere

the glove compartment

the box in the back seat with my nature books, knife, and hand lens

the floor of the shed
my desk there too
the bed
and my head

my other desk
the old couch where no one can sit

inside books
here and there

written on the sand
in Connecticut and Rhode Island

the sketch pad I learned to carry with me

a step at order
but the pages have run out

These are places where my poems live

until I find them.

— Nancy Juretie

THE JOHN BARD TREE

350 years old, we're told. Bard students danced around it
for years and years, picnicking beneath it

> as it grew older and older.

Hollowing out some of its innards, a gang poured gasoline into
those hollows. The tree burned for a week. Much of the trunk
was sacrificed,

> yet its leaves are full on most of the remaining branches.

A small, low chain fence now encircles it, a silent plea for this old
friend, who cannot run away from stupidity, anger, aggression,
the desire to hurt.

For others, the fence stands in reverence, a plaque there now too
reminding all of the days gone past

> the happiness that was
> our stewardship now.

> Nancy Juretie
> Spring
> Bard College
> Annandale-on-Hudson

MEMORY VAPOR
For Adam Paterson

Sitting at one end of a bare
wood table, polished, your
wife, young too, nearby,
cups of tea, cribbage board,
pegs waiting for the first points.

You cradle the deck, shuffle hand
over hand, tap the cards with a satisfying
click, deftly separate them, riffle, flutter,
deal, fan, twist your lips, 'Cut,' you say.
You grin, turning up a six. Skunked me.

Thanksgiving looms. You've made
an appearance since the days of kicking
a ball in leaves crunching with frost, later
years of preparing a vegetarian soup
too concocted to swallow. We tried.

A year ago you had that twenty-four hand,
followed by other high scorers while I limped
far behind with nothing more than a count
of eight. Your wife talked about drinking a gallon
of water a day. Did you try? I did, for a while.

When we gather in a couple of weeks
you will be in our thoughts. Memory: You
hugging me fiercely, the kitchen crowded,
as we tried to accept Bob's death. My brother,
your friend, admirer, close to you, like a father.

If we'd played a game last week, instead
of a year ago . . . if we'd played cribbage,
laughed, talked . . . would you have stolen
the boat, left it to crash onto the shore?
Would you be missing? In the depths . . .

— Nancy Tancredi

MIRAGE

Tree leaned against the air
as if propped by a wall.

I remember when we borrowed
that car, well, stole it, I suppose.

She waved her hands, like maple leaves
in a gust, laughing in a sharp-edged way.

Had to lift her butt up to press the
accelerator, straining to see, cursing
the rain. Windshield was foggy. I wiped it.

Tree lifted the joint to her mouth, sucked,
pulled in her lips, held her breath, tossed
her head back as if that would help the smoke
reach her lungs. Her eyes watered.

The car wasn't such a mess, just the headlight,
well, and fender, and windshield was kinda
cracked. Looked like a spider web. The wall
was cement. We weren't hurt, except for hitting
our heads. Hers was bleeding. I couldn't see it
then, just, she wouldn't move. Her arms hung.
She didn't die. Couldn't talk much though,
still can't. I visit her, help her with the walker.

Gotta go. Who are you by the way?

She peered into the darkness, shrugged. Wrenched
open the door of the old Pontiac, climbed in.

Swerved not to hit a cat. Just like her. Sucker
for animals. Still is. They let her have a cat.

— Nancy Tancredi

CHECK-OUT LINE

Sidelong, soft "I'm sorry."
She fumbles for change,
woman behind her
smiles, waits.

Cloaked in cowering,
pale blond hair stringy,
long enough to be grabbed
by a hand, dirt crusted,
like hers, an open hand
swung in fury, across
right cheek, fisted blow to left,
for years.

Bruises yellowing, eyes swollen,
mascaraed in black,
no teeth - removed two at a time
with a center punch.

She bows her head,
lifts her bag,
glances again at the customer
waiting, mouths, "I'm sorry."

— Nancy Tancredi

PRESCIENCE

Baby birds fluttered into my thoughts. Letters formed into words *P e o p l e d i e*. Clouds of protest arose cackling, cawing, derisive, "Of course of course so what all the time every moment all over the world yes yes people die so what?" The week August kissed September an image insinuated, sharply chiseled memory, doctors, nurses, custodians, striding purposefully, me pushing through the revolving door, engulfed in the scent of fluids and flowers. No reason no reason. Dad had died a year ago. No reason to walk into the Medical Center. *Unless it's my brother.* Emphatic shake of my head. Banish the image. Banish the shadow *Unless it's my brother.* September started its own week, no tag-along August days. A week full of September, for months and months and months.

— Nancy Tancredi

SNOW FENCES

Birch bodies piled on the road's broad
shoulder, leafed heads forced through
the chipper, screeching. Operator, earmuffs
clamped beneath red hard hat, cigarette
smoke a veil, works the gears, keeps the broad
rust-patched trunk aimed at the truck's maw.

Only stumps remain, grove open to scraggly
hackmatacs, needles falling in waning
summer light, curled shavings litter the ground.

Winter will bluster, snow blind drivers, cars
twirl into fledgling blueberry barrens.
Nature's snow fences a mere recollection, or
unknown, to the forgetful, and the young.

— Nancy Tancredi

AUTUMN

Peppering Red, Orange, Gold, Green.
Below the grey Skies
Above my head.
They are catalysts of time.

When the Spirit is inside
The words flow.
When the Spirit is outside awareness,
The words are arrested.

— Patricia Marie Babin

OF NANA AND I

My Nana walked in truth,
She did not always agree,
But she would be the one
To teach respect and dignity

She entrusted these gifts
to each of her own.
Then they in turn could shed
This light to theirs, now grown

As for Nana and I
I felt a special bond
That respect and dignity
Measured rhythms around
My heart sound

She walks in silent truth
The paths of my mind.

— Patricia Marie Babin

TRANQUIL IMAGES

Forty Steps Beach
A personal retreat
Engulfed by its lair
Golden warmth
Salted air.

Surf pounded — rounded rocks
And the vacant, voluminous sea

In peace I seek
The Dove — white dove
Stainless simplicity
Passage not proceeding
Tenderly clutching
The vision.
With delicate melody
To Sustaining its flight
Swinging on wings
In blue light
Of virgin velvet white
Envision the foam
Into edgeless continuity.

— Patricia Marie Babin

THE SHAPE OF DUSK

I sit hunched clutching
a ball point pen in my sweaty palm.
My mind
claws thin air.
I bite my fingers,
cross and uncross my legs, and
blow smoke rings.

I am a diffident
Lilliputian among purposeful Gullivers.
I want to invest heavily
but without struggle.
I fear the contest and doubt the reward.

Scarlet phantasms play across the misty west.
Evening extends its paternal arm.
Vesper bells jangle solemnity.

The choir's last note lingers, falls.
Children end play
trudge homeward to
kitchens lit, embrace of hearths.

Insects mourn the day.
A stream tumbles loudly, now
among stones. The mountain looms.
Surreptitious movement.
Lights blink diminishing.

At the death of day
I enter the tomb of myself,
Groping in ill-lit corridors.

Stars and sleepless eyes
probe the earth's gloom.
A sterile moon,
a naked light bulb.

A firefly, a bush lamp, a searchlight.
The sweep of headlights
and the futility of street lights.
The copper's torch points accusingly.
Illumination fails.

— Peter Anderson

YESTERDAY AND TOMORROW

The shy kiss of new love
And the tender touch of
Raindrops on window pane.

The strong kiss of deep love
And the dripping of sun-melted
Snow from south facing roof.

The sweet kiss of long love
And moonrise and sunset
over steel drums and palm trees.

Fragments of pain, query and tension.
Treasures of joy, sharing and passion.

Open the window, let in the sun,
The flowers, the birdsong,
And the uncertain future.

Love like a chameleon
Scurries erratically forward
To a new time and place.

— Peter Anderson

The Seagull

You wheel over misty ocean swells,
glide over shimmering beaches.
You strain against limits,
scan the sky and sea,
the sandy islands of Vineyard Sound,
the rocky islands of Penobscot Bay
the forests of the Narraguagus
and the coastal towns and villages.

The tern sees you striving and
desires to join your quest.
The osprey sees you straining and
offers assistance.
The cormorant sees you climbing and
warns "you go too far."

The flight yours to make,
the heights yours to seek.
Bound only by the strength of your wings,
the power of your lungs.

The warm southwesterly lifts you upward
to the realm of the sun.
The chill nor'easter drives you inland
to seek refuge.

In a stand of pine a spring
bursts through the ice of an inland pond.
You are warmed, sheltered, renewed.

The storm passes and you rise
on an upward draft to again
seek the realm of the sun.

— Peter Anderson

CONTRAIL

Lying on his back in sweet timothy
he views the thin wisp of steam
in the cloudless sky trailing the passage
from northeast to southwest of the
barely visible vessel bearing
a homeward or outward bound cargo.

Some in jeans or shorts, smartphones in hands
some in business suits, computers in laps.
Families chatter gaily, solo travelers read
books and electronic devices
all intent on their destinations.

He gazes at their trail and then
at a warbler in a nearly tree and the
sparkling water of the cove below.
The dog comes over and lies down beside him.
He doesn't yearn to be any place else.

— Peter Anderson

BUS TO KEY WEST

She boarded the bus at Mile 30,
a stocky black woman with stern expression
locked in contention with Western Union about
sending money to her daughter in Maryland.

Past strip malls with wall to wall
tattoo parlors, fast food joints, loan sharks.
Past tall mangroves blocking the view
of blue water dotted with islands of palms

"I just want to send money to my daughter.
I didn't have any trouble last week sending
money to my sister."

The bus rumbled and rattled and stopped.
A young woman helped an old man with a walker.
Teens glued to their smart phones,
oblivious to the fishermen sharing abandoned
bridges with pelicans.

"I gave them my birthdate;
they didn't ask for an address."
Her voice boomed with irritation through the bus.

Past billboards for tiki bars and fishing trips
past harbors filled with boats,
Past gated communities and chic resorts.

After Hemingway's house and *Sloppy Joes*
and jostling crowds on Spring Break,

We saw her waiting for the return bus
late in the afternoon, asked how she was making out.
She said the money that
her daughter and grandchild needed
still sat in her bank.

— Peter Anderson

EVENING AT BARNEY'S COVE

dusk at the harbor darkening
the water inky blue
with a string of late day clouds
bluing to near black
                           the rose
afterglow deepening beyond
the sunset
             the wind still strong
from the northwest
                  the sea choppy
but its whitecaps no longer
visible
         the winter road to the wharf
glistens
        a fingernail moon shines
while I write

        — Ray N. Beal

WAVES OF GOSSAMER FOG

wing-like fly over the islands
heralding its denser form
as one by one they
are blanketed
                    before the Eastern
Bay becomes obscured, a bright
blue lobster boat finds its way
into the Pig Island Gut
while a dragger is out bound

the fog clears a little
around Sheep but Head Harbor
remains covered
                    it deepens again
does not seem to slow
gulls, nor crows, nor fishermen
in their life's daily chore

— Ray N. Beal

SOMETHING

at the end of the Wohoa Bay
Trail out on the basalt shore
watching the north wind wrinkle
the sea off toward the islands

down to the east the Moosabec Reach
runs under the Jonesport-Beals Bridge
and the houses of the two
settlements cluster the banks
like miniature villages

off to the right along Wohoa shore
my Love, with her dog, gathers
stones and flotsam to create
something never seen before

— Ray N. Beal

"HAIBUN" AT THE BACKFIELD

It is mostly overcast, the sunrays light up Little Sheep Island's skinny camp and one evergreen. While clouds mist on the truck's roof and windshield, the sun spotlights the dome of the retired Bucks Harbor Naval Radar site. As the clouds give way to more blue, the sun shines on the truck, and a pair of sheldrakes glide along the shore of Backfield Cove into the Eastern Bay. The tide has receded by several feet, but the sand is still moist all the way up to the dried grass and dead seaweed at the edge of Nancy's field. A dark hulled lobster boat, seemingly oblivious to the ever rising sea level, pulls its wake by Mark Island into the lower Moosabec Reach. And I sit wondering about my grandchildren's future.

> the line of seaweed
> along the shore rises higher
> the climate warming

— Ray N. Beal

ALMOST . . . ETERNAL

the stalks of bamboo stand as a three
or four foot green and russet army
between a maple and the river
but there is no war here, or is there

the bamboo, not a true bamboo and not
a native, does very well crowding out local
flora with its own version of beauty

upstream on an islet a great black back
gull controls who stays or goes
                                farther up
the flowering wild pear mingling with the new
green of maple and birch while even
farther up, as backdrop, the pine, spruce, and fir
feel reminiscent of Tang Dynasty
landscapes and verses
                        in this world of ideal
words and visions one could almost be eternal

— Ray N. Beal

MY SON

I heard your cry so loud so strong,
My first born son was here!

I touched your little fingers,
Caressed your silky hair.

I kissed you softly on your cheek,
Breathing in your scent so sweet.

I looked into your baby eyes,
Deeply I looked but did not see,
The pain and scars
That would come from me.

I saw, instead, a gift so pure.
A gift from God I'm very sure.

We do not know what life will bring,
I cannot say you did not want for anything.
But you rose above it all, my son,
And I'm so proud you call me Mom.

— Sandra Woodward

AGELESS BEAUTY

Night shift over one last check
On the spunky ninety-seven year old
Who had won my heart.

She was seated on the side of the bed.
As I entered the room,
She queried, "How do I look?"

Dressed in her street clothes
Hair softly framing her face
 Signature red lipstick in place.

My fatigue vanished
As I smiled and replied,
"You are beautiful!"

— Sandra Woodward

STAMP OF DEATH

Majestic white stallion
With golden hooves

You lived your existence in
A relative's dreams

Galloping on swift golden feet
With speed known only
To your breed

A hoof of gold placed
On the chest of an
Ill-fated soul

Over the years Majestic White
You carried out
The people's fate

Until your golden hoof placed
One last time on the teller
Of the dreams.

— Sandra Woodward

ACKNOWLEDGMENTS

Grace Sheridan's "Coats" was previously published in the book *Puffs of Green*; her poem "El Faro" is scheduled for publication in *3 Nations Anthology*.

Joanne Jacob's poem "The Spirit of the Marsh" was published in the periodical *The Catch: Writings from Downeast Maine*."

Peter Anderson's poem "Contrail" was published in the periodical *Jabberwocky*.

Andrea Suarez Hill's poem "Gone" was published in the periodical *The Horses Maine & NH*; her poem "Moonspinner" was published in the periodical *The Aurorean*.

We are grateful to these publications for permission to reprint.

Made in the USA
Middletown, DE
14 January 2019